D1164726

HORSEPOWER

INDY CARS

BY CARRIE A. BRAULICK

CAPSTONE PRESS
a capstone imprint

Blazers Books are published by Capstone Press,
1710 Roe Crest Drive, North Mankato, Minnesota 56003
www.mycapstone.com

Library of Congress Cataloging-in-Publication Data
Library of Congress Cataloging-in-Publication Data is available on the Library of
Congress website.
ISBN: 978-1-5435-2466-6 (library binding)
ISBN: 978-1-5435-2474-1 (paperback)
ISBN: 978-1-5435-2482-6 (eBook PDF)

Summary: This text discusses Indy cars and their unique features.

Editorial Credits
Hank Musolf and Jessica Server, editors; Kyle Grenz, designer; Jo Miller,
media researcher; Kris Wilfahrt, production specialist

Photo Credits
Getty Images: Brian Cleary/Contributor, 25, Icon Sportswire/Contributor, cover;
Newscom: Icon Sportswire 116/Michael Allio, 15, Icon Sportswire DFW/Julian
Avram, 4-5, Sipa USA/Xinhua, 6 (bottom), TNS/Paul Moseley, 16-17, USA
Today Sports/Brian Spurlock, 11, 22-23, USA Today Sports/Mark J. Rebilas, 20,
ZUMA Press/Adam Lacy, 28-29, ZUMA Press/Anatolly Cherkasov, 18, ZUMA
Press/Angel Marchini, 6 (top), ZUMA Press/Chris Young, 9, ZUMA Press/
Michele Sandberg, 13; Shutterstock: HodagMedia, 26

Design Elements
Shutterstock: hugolacasse, khun nay zaw, Shacil

Printed and bound in the United States.
PA017

TABLE OF
CONTENTS

CHAPTER 1

INDY CARS

Indy cars line up behind
the starting line. The flagman
waves a flag. The Indy cars
roar down the racetrack.

Twenty drivers fight for the lead over 85 laps. The competition is fierce. Josef Newgarten's number 2 car has a small lead as the race nears its end.

mechanic—someone who fixes vehicles or machinery

Newgarten holds on to the lead. He takes first place for the second time in the 2017 season!

CHAPTER 2

POWER AND SPEED

Indy cars race at tracks
throughout North America.
The cars are named after the
famous Indianapolis 500 race.

Large V-6 engines power
Indy cars. The engines help the
small cars gain speed quickly.

FAST FACT
<<<<<<<<<<<

Powerful engines help
Indy cars reach 100 miles
(161 kilometers) per hour
in only 4 seconds.

P22 Sens: 2242   PWG Sens: 2247 P..
P22 Offs: 190,2 PWG Offs: 194,9 P..

Indy cars have front and rear **wings**. The wings push air down on the cars. They help the cars grip the track.

wing—a long, flat panel on the front or back of an Indy car

CHAPTER 3

BUILT FOR RACING

Early Indy cars were shaped like boxes. Modern Indy cars are shaped like **bullets**. This shape helps the car travel quickly.

bullet—a small, pointed metal object fired from a gun

Indy cars have smooth tires called **slicks**. The tires wear down during races. At pit crew may replace a car's tires 10 times in one race.

pit stop—a stop that a driver makes during a race to change tires or get fuel

slick—a smooth tire used to race on paved surfaces

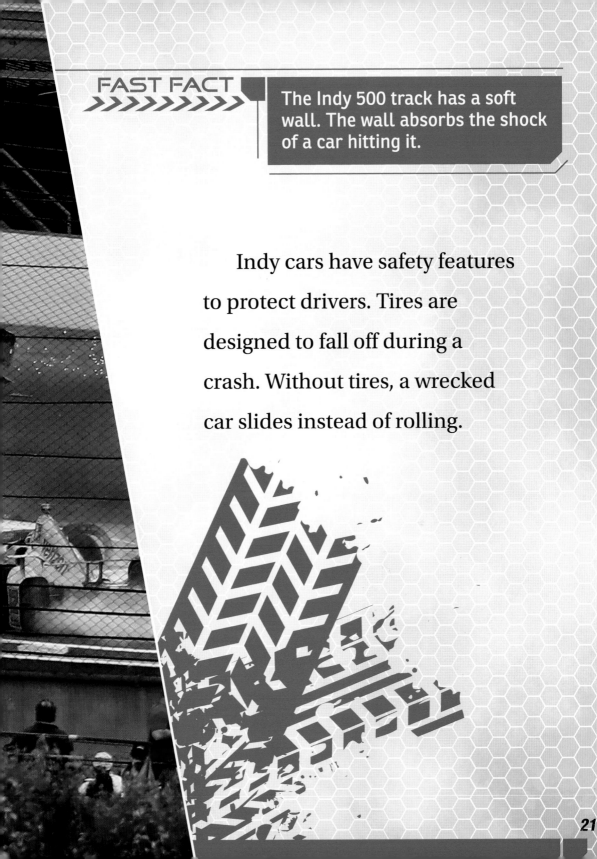

FAST FACT
>>>>>>>>>

The Indy 500 track has a soft wall. The wall absorbs the shock of a car hitting it.

Indy cars have safety features to protect drivers. Tires are designed to fall off during a crash. Without tires, a wrecked car slides instead of rolling.

REAR WING

HONDA

Panasonic

26

TIRE

MOLDED SEAT

INDY CAR DIAGRAM

FRONT WING

CHAPTER 4

INDY CARS IN ACTION

Most races are on large oval-shaped tracks. Other races are on **street courses** through cities.

street course—an Indy car race held on city streets

ND NEW ROADS™

Drivers depend on their cars and teams. Even the best drivers need help from others to win races.

HEADING INTO A TURN

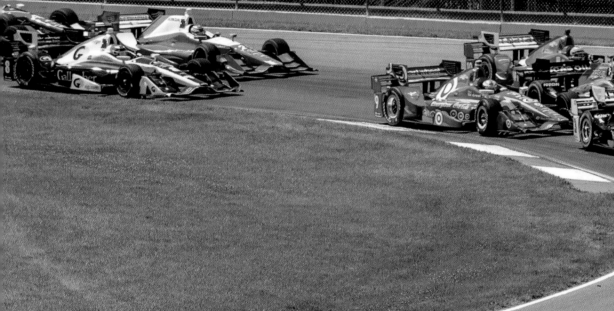

Grandstand 2

GLOSSARY

bullet (BUL-it)— a small, pointed metal object fired from a gun

mechanic (muh-KAN-ik)—someone who fixes vehicles or machinery

pit stop (PIT STOP)—a stop that a driver makes during a race to change tires or get fuel

slick (SLIK)—a smooth tire used to race on paved surfaces

street course (STREET KORSS)—an Indy car race held on city streets

wing (WING)—a long, flat panel on the front or back of an Indy car

READ MORE

Bodensteiner, Peter. *Indy Cars.* Gearhead Garage. Mankato, Minn.: Black Rabbit Books, 2017.

Fishman, Jon M. *Cool Indy Cars.* Awesome Rides. Minneapolis: Lerner Publications, 2019.

Monnig, Alex. *Behind the Wheel of an Indy Car.* In the Driver's Seat. Mankato, Minn.: Childs World, 2016.

INTERNET SITES

Use FactHound to find Internet sites related to this book:

Visit *www.facthound.com*

Just type in 9781543524666 and go.

Check out projects, games and lots more at
www.capstonekids.com

INDEX